WHAT WE STAND FOR

KEEPING THE
PEACE

the kids' book of
PEACEMAKING

ANDERS HANSON

CONSULTING EDITOR, DIANE CRAIG, M.A./READING SPECIALIST

Super Sandcastle

An Imprint of Abdo Publishing
www.abdopublishing.com

visit us at www.abdopublishing.com

Published by Abdo Publishing, a division of ABDO, PO Box 398166, Minneapolis, Minnesota 55439.
Copyright © 2015 by Abdo Consulting Group, Inc. International copyrights reserved in all countries.
No part of this book may be reproduced in any form without written permission from the publisher.
Super SandCastle™ is a trademark and logo of Abdo Publishing.

Printed in the United States of America, North Mankato, Minnesota
062014
092014

THIS BOOK CONTAINS
RECYCLED MATERIALS

Editor: Liz Salzmann
Content Developer: Nancy Tuminelly
Cover and Interior Design and Production: Mighty Media, Inc.
Photo Credits: Shutterstock

Library of Congress Cataloging-in-Publication Data

Hanson, Anders, 1980-
  Keeping the peace : the kids' book of peacemaking / Anders Hanson ; consulting Editor, Diane
Craig, M.A., Reading Specialist.
       pages cm. -- (What we stand for)
  ISBN 978-1-62403-294-3
1. Conflict management--Juvenile literature. 2. Interpersonal conflict--Juvenile literature.
3. Interpersonal relations--Juvenile literature. I. Title.
  HM1126.H3564 2015
  303.6'9--dc23
                        2013041838

Super SandCastle™ books are created by a team of professional educators, reading specialists, and
content developers around five essential components—phonemic awareness, phonics, vocabulary, text
comprehension, and fluency—to assist young readers as they develop reading skills and strategies and
increase their general knowledge. All books are written, reviewed, and leveled for guided reading, early
reading intervention, and Accelerated Reader® programs for use in shared, guided, and independent
reading and writing activities to support a balanced approach to literacy instruction.

CONTENTS

WHAT IS
PEACEMAKING?

Peacemaking is
helping others
to get along.

Grant tries to
take Ellie's bear.

5

People have
disagreements.

A peacemaker is
someone who turns
disagreements into
agreements!

Jada hits Sofia
with a pillow.

First, have each person talk about the problem.

Listen to what both people say. Don't interrupt.
Let them say everything they need to say.

Find out what caused the problem.

Suggest win-win **solutions**. A win-win solution is one that each person feels good about. Everybody wins!

WHAT CAN YOU DO?

How can you be a peacemaker?

"WHAT DO YOU WANT?"

Many disagreements are caused by misunderstandings. Have both people say clearly what they want.

"HOW DO YOU FEEL?"

It's okay to feel sad or hurt. But it's important to **express** those feelings in a positive way.

Kevin is hurt. Ivan and Cooper won't share the game. He tells them how he feels.

"WHY DO YOU FEEL THAT WAY?"

Everybody's feelings are important. It's good to know why someone feels the way they do. Ask both people to say why they feel that way

Jada listens to Sophia explain how she feels.

"SUM UP WHAT THE OTHER PERSON SAID."

Make you understand each other. Have each person **repeat** what the other said.

Derek repeats what Trevor said. He wants to be sure he understands Trevor's feelings.

SUGGEST PLANS WITH WIN-WIN SOLUTIONS.

Think of ways to **solve** the problem. Are there **solutions** that make both people happy?

WHAT WILL YOU DO?

What is one thing you can do to be a peacemaker?

GLOSSARY

EXPRESS – to make your feelings or thoughts known through words or actions.

REPEAT – to do or say something again.

SOLUTION – an answer to, or a way to solve, a problem.

SOLVE – to find an answer, explanation, or solution.